CONVERSATIONS WITH Jesus

Intimate Snapshots

Martha Reapsome

8 Discussions for Group Bible Study

Neighborhood Bible Studies Publishers
56 Main Street
Dobbs Ferry, NY 10522
1-800-369-0307
email: nbstudies@aol.com
www.NeighborhoodBibleStudy.org

GROUP PARTICIPANTS

Name	Address	Phone Number

Scripture quotations, unless otherwise indicated, are taken from the HOLY BIBLE, NEW INTERNATIONAL VERSION®. Copyright © 1973, 1978, 1984 by International Bible Society. Used by permission of Zondervan Publishing House. All rights reserved.

All rights reserved. No part of this book may be reproduced or transmitted in any form or by any means, electronic or mechanical, including photocopying, recording, or any information storage and retrieval system without written permission from Neighborhood Bible Studies, 56 Main Street, Dobbs Ferry, New York, 10522; 1-800-369-0307; nbstudies@aol.com

Copyright ©2005, 2001 by Martha Reapsome

ISBN 1-880266-37-7
Second printing 2005
Printed in the United States of America
Cover photo by Fran Goodrich

Contents

How To Use this Discussion Guide	4
INTRODUCTION	7
Discussion 1 *Mark 1:21-39* THE COMMUNITY AND FRIENDS	9
Discussion 2 *John 4:1-30* THE THIRSTY	14
Discussion 3 *Luke 7:36-50 & Mark 7:1-23* THE SELF RIGHTEOUS	20
Discussion 4 *Mark 10:17-31* MATERIALISTS	25
Discussion 5 *John 9:1-41* THE BLIND	30
Discussion 6 *Mark 9:30-37; 10:32-45* THE "ME FIRST" PEOPLE	36
Discussion 7 *Luke 23:1-25, 32-49* MOCKERS, ACCUSERS AND JUDGE	41
Discussion 8 *John 20:1-31* DISTRESSED FRIENDS AND A DOUBTER	46
WHAT SHOULD OUR GROUP STUDY NEXT?	51

HOW TO USE THIS DISCUSSION GUIDE

This study guide uses the inductive approach to Bible study. It will help you discover for yourself what the Bible says. It will not give you prepackaged answers. People remember most what they discover for themselves and what they express in their own words. The study guide provides three kinds of questions:
1. What does the passage say? What are the facts?
2. What is the meaning of these facts?
3. How does this passage apply to your life?

- Observe the facts carefully before you interpret the meaning of your observations. Then apply the truths you have discovered to life today. Resist the temptation to skip the fact questions since we are not as observant as we think. Find the facts quickly so you can spend more time on their meaning and application.

- *The purpose of Bible study is not just to know more Bible truths but to apply them.* Allow these truths to make a difference in how you think and act, in your attitudes and relationships, in the quality and direction of your life.

- Each discussion requires about one hour. Decide on the amount of time to add for socializing and prayer.

- *Share the leadership.* If a different person is the moderator or question-asker each week, interest grows and members feel the group belongs to everyone. The Bible is the authority in the group, not the question-asker.

- When a group grows to more than ten, the quiet people become quieter. Plan to grow and multiply. You can meet as two groups in the same house or begin another group so that more people can participate and benefit.

TOOLS FOR AN EFFECTIVE BIBLE STUDY

1. A study guide for each person in the group.
2. A modern translation of the Bible such as:
    New International Version (NIV)
    Contemporary English Version (CEV)
    Jerusalem Bible (JB)
    New American Standard Bible (NASB)
    Revised English Bible (REB)
    New Revised Standard Version (NRSV)
3. An English dictionary.
4. A map of the Lands of the Bible in a Bible or in the study guide.
5. Your conviction that the Bible is worth studying.

GUIDELINES FOR AN EFFECTIVE STUDY

1. Stick to the passage under discussion.
2. Avoid tangents. If the subject is not addressed in the passage, put it on hold until after the study.
3. Let the Bible speak for itself. Do not quote other authorities or rewrite it to say what you want it to say.
4. Apply the passage personally and honestly.
5. Listen to one another to sharpen your insights.
6. Prepare by reading the Bible passage and thinking through the questions during the week.
7. Begin and end on time.

HELPS FOR THE QUESTION-ASKER

1. Prepare by reading the passage several times, using different translations if possible. Ask for God's help in understanding it. Consider how the questions might be answered. Observe which questions can be answered quickly and which may require more time.

2. Begin on time.

3. Lead the group in opening prayer or ask someone ahead of time to do so. Don't take anyone by surprise.

4. Ask for a different volunteer to read each Bible section. Read the question. Wait for an answer. Rephrase the question if necessary. Resist the temptation to answer the question yourself. Move to the next question. Skip questions already answered by the discussion.

5. Encourage everyone to participate. Ask the group, "What do the rest of you think?" "What else could be added?"

6. Receive all answers warmly. If needed, ask, "In which verse did you find that?" "How does that fit with verse...?"

7. If a tangent arises, ask, "Do we find the answer to that here?" Or suggest, "Let's write that down and look for the information as we go along."

8. Discourage members who are too talkative by saying, "When I read the next question, let's hear from someone who hasn't spoken yet today."

9. Use the summary questions to bring the study to a conclusion on time.

10. Close the study with prayer.

11. Decide on one person to be the host and another person to ask the questions at the next discussion.

Introduction to Conversations With Jesus

What is history but the stories of people from the beginning of recorded time? Stories show us the personality, character, strengths and weaknesses of people. We learn something about George Washington from the story of the American Revolutionary War Battle of Trenton. He took his entire army across the icy Delaware River by night to surprise and defeat the British forces at Trenton and Princeton.

How can we get to know Jesus, a man who lived centuries ago? In the same way—by reading stories about his life and listening in to conversations he had. The four New Testament Gospels, biographies of Jesus, give eyewitness accounts of his life. The studies in this guide give you the opportunity to put yourself into the setting, action, and emotions of the people who met Jesus.

Take time to imagine the setting. Observe Jesus. Listen to him; feel his emotions; sense others' reactions to him. Allow yourself to relive the drama as if you were one of the characters within it. Discover for yourself who Jesus is, what he did, and why he came. Watch him break down ethnic, social and gender barriers.

Whether this Bible study is your first or your hundredth, you can discover more about Jesus. Discussing the stories of Jesus with friends sharpens your insights and enriches your understanding of him.

After living with Jesus for three years, the Apostle John wrote that Jesus came from the Father, full of grace and truth (John 1:14). We don't usually associate graciousness with truth. We like to be treated graciously, but a person who "tells it like it is" seldom does it graciously. We value truthfulness, but may hate to hear truth about ourselves. Watch for this unique blend of qualities in Jesus as you examine these stories. Consider how Jesus wants to bring graciousness and truth to your life.

DISCUSSION 1

The Community and Friends

MARK 1:21-39

A leader must communicate his vision clearly and use his authority wisely to attract followers. If he demonstrates power with compassion he draws more followers.

1. What qualities do you admire in a leader?

At about age 30, Jesus left his carpenter shop in Nazareth and began to preach, "The time has come. The kingdom of God is near. Repent and believe the good news." As he traveled along the Sea of Galilee, he chose Simon, Andrew, James and John, four commercial fishermen to be his first disciples. Jesus' brief stay in Capernaum demonstrates his authority, power, and compassion. But it also brings conflict between Jesus' priorities and his friends' wishes.

READ MARK 1:21-28

2. When Jesus teaches in the synagogue, why does his teaching amaze the people?

3. What else amazes them in the synagogue that morning?

4. Why would Jesus silence the evil spirit who knows who he is?

5. If you had been in the synagogue that morning, what are the main things you would tell your friends who had not been there?

READ MARK 1:29-34

6. When Simon and his friends arrive home from the synagogue service, what do they find?

7. What do you learn about Jesus from the way the disciples and Jesus handle the problem?

8. How does the news of Jesus' authority and power affect the whole town?

Note: Jewish law prohibited carrying anything or walking unnecessarily on the Sabbath, from sunset Friday till sunset Saturday.

9. What impresses you about the way Jesus uses his power and authority?

How does Jesus differ from other teachers the people of Capernaum know?

READ MARK 1:35-39

10. After his eventful Sabbath and evening, where does Jesus go and when?

Why do you think he does this?

11. Why do Simon and his companions go looking for Jesus?

Why, do you think, do the people want Jesus to return to town?

12. Imagine yourself in this situation. Your friends and neighbors admire you and want you to keep doing something good for them. You must choose either to please your friends or to stick to your higher priority. How would you decide what to do?

13. What does Jesus reveal about his purpose and priorities?

14. Jesus was choosing, not between good and evil, but between good and best. Why is this always a difficult choice?

15. What does verse 39 indicate about Jesus' compassion as he pursues his purpose of preaching in other places?

REFLECTION

1. From this study, what attracts you to or disturbs you about Jesus?

2. Jesus knew the purpose of his life and set his priorities accordingly. In later studies you'll discover

more about his purpose. How does having a purpose in life or lack of a purpose affect how you live?

CONCLUSION

Jesus amazed the people in Capernaum with his teaching, his authority over demons, and his ability to heal various diseases. How convenient it would have been to stay in Capernaum where he was warmly received, and where he was welcomed into the home of his disciples. Jesus knew why he was here. Clear about his priorities, Jesus preached everywhere he went and relieved peoples' physical needs.

As you reflect on what you learned about Jesus in this passage you may want to tell him about the areas of your life that need his healing touch. You may want to ask for wisdom and courage to choose the best, even when others pressure you to settle for less.

DISCUSSION 2

The Thirsty

JOHN 4:1-30

Can you remember a time when you were so thirsty that you thought you would collapse? Human beings cannot survive physically without water. Look at all the ways we try to satisfy our physical thirst. We carry water bottles on the train, to ball games, to meetings, on hikes, in the car, even in church. Have you counted the beverage aisles in your grocery store? Satisfying our physical thirst is obviously a high priority in order to stay healthy. Satisfying our inner spiritual and emotional thirst may not be as obvious, but it is of equally high priority for spiritual health. We desperately need the water of life Jesus has to offer.

1. What are some of the constructive and destructive ways people try to satisfy their spiritual and emotional thirsts today?

In Jesus' day there was much prejudice between Jews and Samaritans. The antagonism was so great that Jewish travelers walked extra miles to avoid entering Samaria. Centuries earlier the Assyrians had conquered the Jews, deported most of them, and intermarried with the Jews remaining in the land. The Jews of Jesus' day considered Samaritans impure traitors so they would not speak to Samaritans—would not even touch their utensils. Notice how Jesus breaks down ethnic and gender barriers to reach one thirsty woman.

READ JOHN 4:1-30

2. What impresses you about Jesus from verses 4-8?

Note: The sixth hour would be noon. Women usually came to the well in the cooler early morning to get water, visit, and share the news of the town.

Have two people read the conversation in verses 7-26.

3. Why is the woman shocked at Jesus' request for a drink?

4. How does Jesus arouse her curiosity and interest (verses 10-15)?

In what ways does the living water Jesus offers differ from the physical water in the well?

5. Why does the woman ask for the water Jesus talks about (verse 15)?

How does this differ from Jesus' reason for offering it (verses 10, 13, 18)?

6. Jesus wanted to do more for this woman than eliminate her daily walk to the well. Why does Jesus want to do more for us than simply changing our circumstances?

7. When the Samaritan woman asks for the living water, how does Jesus change the subject (verse 16)?

   Think of what may have led this woman into a lifestyle of multiple marriages. What do you think she was seeking, dreaming of, really wanting?

   How is Jesus offering to meet her deeper needs?

8. How does the woman avoid talking about her personal life (verses 19, 20)?

   What are some current religious questions we use to avoid thinking about our personal spiritual thirst?

9. What does it mean to you to realize that Jesus takes the woman's religious questions seriously and graciously uses them to meet her deeper needs?

How does Jesus use the woman's question to help her understand more about God and about true worship (verses 21-26)?

Note: Messiah or Christ refers to the special deliverer God promised to send to his people.

10. Jesus' twelve disciples are learning more about him as they watch his life and listen to him, but he has not yet identified himself to anyone. Why do you think Jesus chooses this woman as the first person to whom he announces who he is?

11. When the disciples return, what do they see and how do they react (verse 27)?

12. How are the woman's actions in verses 28 and 29 evidence that she believes Jesus and has accepted his offer of living water?

How does believing in Jesus—drinking the living water—satisfy the woman's thirst for acceptance and security?

REFLECTION

1. Why do the spiritually and emotionally thirsty, in Jesus' day and today, need both the graciousness and the truth that Jesus brings?

2. Think about the dissatisfactions you feel and the ways you try to relieve them. Perhaps your search, like the Samaritan woman's, brings disapproval and rejection from others. Or you may search in socially acceptable but equally futile ways. What do you learn about Jesus from this story that encourages you to consider his offer of living water that can permanently satisfy your thirst for forgiveness, acceptance, eternal life?

3. If you have already experienced this living water, how would you describe the ways it satisfies your thirst?

CONCLUSION

Jesus breaks through cultural, social and religious barriers to bring living water to the thirsty. Jesus treats the Samaritan woman with respect though he knows all about her. He patiently arouses her curiosity and gives her the opportunity to learn more about him. The lives of many around us, perhaps even our own lives, betray our empty efforts to satisfy a thirst for acceptance, forgiveness, and security.

Consider how refreshing and satisfying it is to receive a gracious gift of attention and respect from Jesus who knows the whole truth about you.

DISCUSSION 3

The Self Righteous

LUKE 7:36-50 AND MARK 7:1-23

Think about the ways some people defend their self-image:
"I live a good life doing the best I can."
"I'm no worse than the next guy and I'm better than most."
"In the end I think my good deeds will outweigh the bad ones."
"I try to keep the Ten Commandments."
"Basically, I'm a good person. I've never hurt anyone."

Think about the ways other people put themselves down:
"I blew it again. I don't think there is any hope for me."
"I just can't get my life together."
"I know I'll never amount to anything."
"God wouldn't want to have anything to do with me."

1. Why is it hard for us to get a balanced picture of ourselves?

The Pharisees were a group of Jewish religious leaders who believed that strictly obeying the law made them righteous. The law included God's commandments plus thousands of regulations the rabbis added over the years. They believed that God accepted them because they kept all these rules and avoided contact with anything unclean. They believed that their own efforts could make them acceptable to God. They certainly would not associate with sinners—immoral people who did not keep the laws.

In today's story, a Pharisee named Simon invites Jesus to dinner. Picture the setting: a low banquet table surrounded by couches where the guests recline, leaning on their elbows with their feet extended behind them. A religious host often allowed poor people in to listen to the discussion. However, they were expected to stand quietly in the back and not make any trouble.

READ LUKE 7:36-50

2. Why do you think Simon invites Jesus to dinner and then neglects the courtesies a host commonly shows to a guest (verses 44-46)?

3. How does Simon compare himself to Jesus?

4. Imagine you are the woman. What do you think of Jesus? (verses 37, 38, 44-48)

5. What does it cost this woman emotionally, financially, and socially, to demonstrate her love to Jesus?

6. Why does Jesus tell Simon the story? (verses 39-42)

7. What is Jesus saying here about sin and forgiveness? Jesus again clashes with the Pharisees over their different definitions of righteousness and sin. In Mark 7 the confrontation highlights their different answers to: Where does sin begin, inside or outside us? How does one obtain forgiveness and a clean start?

READ MARK 7:1-23

8. According to the Pharisees what makes a person a sinner (verses 1-5)?

9. What does Jesus say makes a person a sinner (verses 6-8 and 14-23)?

10. In what ways can we substitute our traditions or cultural ideas for God's commands?

Why can't external rituals change our sinful hearts?

What surprises or impresses you in Jesus' list of sins (verses 21-23)?

11. According to Jesus, why are all people sinners who need forgiveness?

REFLECTION

1. What impresses you about how Jesus brings graciousness to Simon and to the woman?

   What truth does Jesus bring to those who think they are good enough and to those who know they need forgiveness?

2. Simon's self-righteousness came when he compared himself to another person and concluded that he was not a sinner. How can we gain an accurate picture of our true spiritual condition?

3. Imagine Jesus saying to you, as he did to the woman in Simon's house, "Your sins are forgiven. Your faith has saved you; go in peace." How would you want to respond to him?

   What may it cost you?

CONCLUSION

Jesus accepted a dinner invitation from a proud, prejudiced, self-righteous man. He graciously helped the man, Simon, to face the truth about himself. Jesus' treatment of the woman known to have lived a sinful life was equally frank and gracious. Jesus claimed to have the power and authority to forgive sinners, the moral and the immoral. He graciously accepted the woman's tears, kisses, and perfume as gifts of love and gratitude.

Does it pain you to read Jesus' list of what comes out of a person's heart? Recognizing your sin makes you eligible for forgiveness and prepares you to respond to Jesus out of love for him.

If you are ready to do this, you may wish to take a few minutes to silently ask God's forgiveness for the things in this list that you find in your own heart.

DISCUSSION 4

Materialists

MARK 10:17-31

Advertisements expose what our culture values.
"Make every day delicious." Fancy Feast cat food.
"Now your kitchen will stand out. (Instead of your refrigerator.)"
"A luxury sedan with plenty of curb appeal."
"How much is enough?"
"You deserve a break today."
Houses, comfort, luxury, pets, and financial security consume our energy and fill our dreams.

Humans are by nature acquisitive and self-seeking. Add that to our consumer culture, and we are all in danger of being materialistic. According to the dictionary, a materialist is a person who is markedly more concerned about material things than about spiritual values.

1. Why is it easy to be a materialist no matter what your income level?

In Jesus' day, the Jewish people believed that wealth was a reward from God to a righteous person, so the wealthy, moral Jewish man in this study could be very pleased about God's approval. Yet he approaches Jesus with a personal spiritual question.

READ MARK 10:17-31

2. What do you learn about the man who comes to Jesus in verses 17-22?

3. From what you have discovered about Jesus in the earlier studies, why might the man bring this question to Jesus?

4. What are the two subjects in Jesus' answer (verses 18, 19)?

   How are both relevant to the man's question?

Note: The commandments—refers to the Ten Commandments given by God to Moses to set as a standard for the Jewish people. When Jesus speaks about the commandments, he lists only those dealing with behavior toward other people. He does not mention the commandments about a person's relationship to God. See Exodus 20:1-17.

5. Read the man's reply in verse 20 with the tone of voice and emotions you think he used.

6. Though this man keeps certain commandments, he still lacks something. What four things does Jesus ask him to do (verse 21)?

What promise does Jesus make to him if he obeys?

7. There is no record that Jesus asked any other person to sell everything to follow him. Why does Jesus make the cost so high for this potential follower?

   Why is counting the cost necessary for any potential follower of Jesus?

8. Why do you think the man does not accept the offer to be one of Jesus' followers?

9. The man went away sad. From verses 21-23 what emotions do you think Jesus feels here?

   Why is it hard for a rich person to enter the kingdom of heaven?

10. In contrast to this rich man, what does Peter claim?

11. What does Jesus promise to every person who values the kingdom of God more than anything else?

How does this promise affect the way you look at your relationships and possessions?

REFLECTION

1. In what ways does Jesus disturb or encourage you in this conversation?

2. This rich, moral man still needed one thing to enter the kingdom of God. He had to rid himself of what he valued more than God. If Jesus said to you, "You still lack one thing…," think about what that thing might be for you.

3. This man asks how to inherit eternal life (verse 17); Jesus talks about entering the kingdom of God (verse 23). Others ask about who can be saved (verse 26). Jesus promises eternal life to those who forsake all for the kingdom of God for him and the gospel (verse 29). How do these phrases help you understand what Jesus offers?

   How is what Jesus offers more valuable than anything you own?

CONCLUSION

Jesus patiently yet forthrightly guides this rich man to see the truth about himself. He directs him to look to God for the standard of goodness. Jesus commands the rich man to give up his self-sufficiency and pride to put God first.

We, too, can fail to see our sins of self-sufficiency and pride. It is easy for us to depend on our jobs, education, bank accounts, or retirement plans for security. We may put more value on our comfort and power and prestige than on the kingdom of God. It is far too easy to believe that what we see is more valuable and lasting than what we cannot see. What a comfort to know that Jesus offers us forgiveness and the grace to rid ourselves of whatever we value more than we value him.

As you reflect on this man's conversation with Jesus, you may want examine your ideas of goodness and self-sufficiency. You may want to tell Jesus how you feel about his demands or his promises.

DISCUSSION 5

The Blind

JOHN 9:1-41

*"Who is so deaf or so blind as is he,
That willfully will not hear or see?"*
John Haywood (1497-1580)

The physically blind live in darkness, the absence of light. They grope, or stumble easily. They can't see physical reality like where the bus stops, where the meat is on the plate, how many people are in the room, the colors of the garden or the baby's eyes. To compensate they develop keen hearing and sensitive touch. To walk they must depend on a white cane, a guide dog, the shoulder and eyes of another person. They know they cannot see.

The spiritually blind also live in darkness, the absence of light. They grope, or stumble easily. They can't see spiritual reality like the truth about God, themselves and the world. To compensate they develop strong opinions, a confidence in tradition, education or their own wisdom. The only difference is that they think they can "see".

1. Recall a time when you looked at a situation or read an article and did not "see" what friends around you saw or understood. How did their insights make you feel? Did you want to pretend you saw what they did, or did you argue about their ideas?

While Jesus is in Jerusalem for the Feast of Tabernacles (John 7-8), he makes very bold claims, such as "God is my Father." "I am the light of the world." In today's study, Jewish leaders question him about these claims. A debate rages among the religious elite and the people about who Jesus really is. At one point some take up stones to kill him. In this atmosphere, as Jesus walks through the crowded city with his disciples, he notices a man blind from birth.

READ JOHN 9:1-12
SCENE 1, THE MIRACLE

2. Who are the characters in the opening scene?

The Jews in that day believed that sin caused illness. How does a man born blind create a dilemma for the disciples?

3. What surprises you about Jesus' answer (verses 3, 4)?

4. Earlier Jesus had healed a paralyzed man by commanding him to walk. He had healed a leper by simply touching him. Why do you think Jesus involves the blind man in this healing?

5. If you were this blind man, what is it in Jesus' voice, words, manner, or touch that causes you to do what he says?

What would the walk home and the neighbors' questions be like for you?

READ JOHN 9:13-34
SCENE 2, THE INTERROGATION

6. Why do the Pharisees and the healed man have different opinions of Jesus (verses 13-17)?

Note: One of the ten commandments is "Remember the Sabbath Day to keep it holy." Over the years the rabbis had added many specific restrictions to the command. Do not carry anything, do no work, do not knead dough and by extension, clay. Keeping such regulations was the acid test of a righteous person.

7. How do the man's parents handle the pressure of the Pharisees' questions and threats (verses 18-23)?

Note: The synagogue was the congregation of God's people, the center of education and social contacts. Anyone excluded from the synagogue would be ostracized by the community.

8. Read the dialogue in verses 24-34 with a narrator, the healed man, and a Pharisee.

What is the healed man able to see that the Pharisees can't? Why?

Note: The phrase, Give glory to God, places the healed man under a solemn oath to tell the truth.

9. The man's irrefutable testimony frustrates his questioners (verse 25).

What do you learn from his example about how to answer those who question you about Jesus?

10. How do the Pharisees act out their blindness in verses 28, 34?

11. Imagine the healed man's emotional roller coaster ride. The joy of seeing! Interrogated by neighbors and religious leaders. Insulted and expelled from the synagogue. What do you think he is feeling after all of this?

READ JOHN 9:35-41
SCENE 3, THE CONFRONTATION

12. Put yourself in the healed man's shoes in this scene. What would it mean to you to be found by Jesus (verse 35)?

13. Trace the man's understanding of who Jesus is in verses 11, 17, 25, 30-33, 35-38.

    How does this conversation lead him to worship Jesus?

Note: Son of Man is a title for an exalted figure who will serve as judge at the end of history.

REFLECTION

1. What attitudes and actions lead to the Pharisees' spiritual blindness (verses 16, 24, 28, 29, 34, 40, 41)?

    What current attitudes and values can blind us spiritually to the truth about Jesus?

    How can you avoid these?

2. Jesus revealed his compassion, power, and identity to the blind man. He revealed their spiritual blindness to the Pharisees. What new under-standing of Jesus have you gained from this study?

What new understanding of yourself have you gained?

How is learning either of these truths a gracious gift to you?

CONCLUSION

Jesus notices one blind beggar among the crowd in the city. He uses this person's handicap to bring glory to God. The once-blind man's growing conviction that the one who healed him must be from God stands in stark contrast to the stubborn refusal of the Pharisees to see this truth.

We, too, are susceptible to the spiritual blindness of the Pharisees. Our culture presents us with many lies and false assumptions about Jesus. From this study we see that Jesus wants to rescue us from willful blindness and open our eyes to the truth.

You may want to ask him for the courage to believe him. Or you may ask him to help you speak clearly and boldly, like the healed man, about what he has done in your life.

DISCUSSION 6

The "Me First" People

MARK 9:30-37; 10: 32-45

A five-year-old boy runs to the front of the line. He wants to be first. Onlookers may smile thinking, "That's how five year olds are." But what about adults who always need to be first? Most of us resent people who push their own importance. Name-droppers and status seekers, competing to be at the top of the social pecking order, are often oblivious to how annoying they can be. We easily recognize pride in others. Later we discover that what we dislike in others is usually what we dislike most about ourselves.

1. In what situations are you tempted to push your own importance?

For almost three years the disciples listen to Jesus teach, see his miracles, marvel at his acceptance of the nobodies in their culture, and observe his confrontations with religious leaders. Twice Jesus sends his disciples out with power to preach and to heal. He waits for them to figure out that he is the Messiah, God's promised deliverer. When they do, he is on his way to Jerusalem for the last time. The disciples anticipate Jesus establishing his kingdom, and over-throwing the Romans. Feel the tension as Jesus leads the disciples toward Jerusalem.

READ MARK 9:30-37

2. Why does Jesus want to be alone with his disciples (verses 30-32)?

How do the disciples react to Jesus' shocking announcement?

Note: Son of Man is the name Jesus used in referring to himself. It emphasizes his humanity, becoming one of us. In the Old Testament, Son of Man referred to the one with authority and power who would come from God (Daniel 7:13-14).

3. While Jesus anticipates his death, what is on the disciples' minds?

4. Imagine telling your friends you are about to die and they start to argue about which one is your best friend. What would you feel and do?

How does Jesus handle this similar situation?

5. What does Jesus want his "me first" disciples to understand about honor and greatness in his kingdom (verses 35-37)?

READ MARK 10:32-45

6. As they travel toward Jerusalem some time later, Jesus returns to the same subject. What details does he add this time (verses 32-34)?

   What would it be like for you to know the details of how and when you will die?

7. How do you account for the behavior of James and John in verses 35-39?

   How does Jesus answer their request?

8. What evidence is there that the other disciples are no better than James and John in their attitudes (verses 41-45)?

9. Give a current illustration of our society's idea of how to demonstrate greatness?

10. In contrast to the ways rulers of the Gentiles behave, how must people act who want to become great and to be first in Jesus' kingdom?

Think of some leaders you have had at work, on committees, or in your community. How do their characteristics compare to the characteristics Jesus requires?

11. What reasons does Jesus give for his life and death (verse 45)?

12. A ransom is the release of a hostage in return for a price. Sometimes one person will take the place of the hostage.

How does that help you understand the purpose of Jesus' death?

REFLECTION

1. From the previous studies give examples of Jesus living out his definition of greatness.

2. Jesus knew who he was, where he came from, and where he was going so he humbly and confidently served. How has your self-knowledge in these areas grown and changed from studying these six conversations with Jesus?

3. What impresses you about the way Jesus graciously brings truth to proud, "me first" people?

CONCLUSION

Jesus patiently taught his proud disciples about position and protocol in his kingdom. He fleshed out his principles by graciously serving the somebodies and the nobodies in his world. Jesus demonstrated true greatness in his day-to-day experiences, and ultimately in giving his life as a ransom for all the proud, "me first" people of the world, including us.

We often find it hard to serve even those who are kind to us. How much harder it is to serve those who are proud or self-seeking. Knowing Jesus can help us begin to understand who we are and where we are going. With this understanding we are better equipped to serve.

You may want to ask Jesus to convince you of how important each one of us is to him. You may ask him to open your eyes to see the opportunities to serve others as an expression of your gratitude to him.

DISCUSSION 7

Mockers, Accusers and Judge

LUKE 23:1-25, 32-49

Many of us have bad childhood memories of the cruel taunts we received on the playground or nicknames the bigger kids called us. We were told that "sticks and stones may break my bones, but words will never hurt me." But mocking words do hurt us, often with wounds more than skin deep.

Even now as adults, whispered rumors or false accusations can still intimidate us. A soccer coach was once falsely accused of molesting a girl in his office. He was coaching an away game the day the girl said it happened. But before all the facts came out, he was fired, declared guilty in the local paper, and shunned by the community. Eventually he was cleared of all charges, but not rehired. The power of false and mocking words is indeed strong.

1. Recall a time when someone mocked or falsely accused you. What did you want to do in response? What did you do?

Jesus knew what it was like to be falsely accused. One of his disciples, Judas, betrayed Jesus to the Jewish authorities. The chief priests and teachers of the law questioned him about his claim to be the Son of God. When Jesus said they were right in saying he was the Son of God, they angrily hurried their prisoner to Pilate, the Roman governor. Only the Romans had the power to execute a criminal and the Jewish elders wanted Jesus put to death.

THE TRIAL
READ LUKE 23:1-25
SCENE 1, BEFORE PILATE

2. Imagine this scene, and the accusers accompanying the prisoner into Pilate's courtroom. What do you hear in their voices and see in their body language (verses 1-5)?

3. What charges do they bring against Jesus (verses 2-5)?

4. What does Pilate think of the charges (verses 1-4)?

SCENE 2, BEFORE HEROD

5. Describe the interrogation, accusations and mocking in Herod's court (verses 8-12).

SCENE 3, BEFORE PILATE AGAIN

6. What impresses you about Pilate's verdict and actions in verses 13-16?

7. What statement about Jesus does Pilate repeat three times (verses 4, 14, 22)?

8. What impresses you about the choices the accusers and Pilate make in verses 16-25?

   What influences the choices that people make about Jesus today?

Note: It was the custom at Passover to release a prisoner to please the people.

THE CRUCIFIXION
READ LUKE 23:32-43
SCENE 1

9. The soldiers lead Jesus and two other criminals out of the city to a hill shaped like a skull. Picture the crowd of spectators, the rulers, the soldiers, and the criminals surrounding Jesus. With what words and actions does each group mock Jesus?

   Today, what do people say, write, or do to mock Jesus?

10. How do you account for the different attitudes of the two criminals toward Jesus (verses 39-43)?

What do you learn about Jesus' power and kingdom from his response to the repentant criminal?

11. What words would you use to describe Jesus in this scene (verses 34 and 43 especially)?

READ LUKE 23: 44–49
SCENE 2

Note: The sixth hour to the ninth hour would be from noon to three p.m.

In the temple, a long, thick curtain separated the Most Holy Place from the worshippers. Only the High priest could enter the presence of God, once a year when he brought the blood of a sacrifice for sin. Other Gospel accounts record that the curtain was torn from the top down.

12. What do the unusual events and Jesus' last words reveal about him (verses 44–46)?

13. What different reactions do the centurion, the spectators, and the women have to Jesus' death? Why?

Note: The centurion, a Roman commander of one hundred soldiers, would have watched many men die.

14. In what different ways do people today react to Jesus' death, and why?

REFLECTION

1. Surrounded by mockers and accusers, how does Jesus demonstrate that he is in control of events in his trial and death?

2. In what ways does Jesus bring graciousness and truth even in his trial and death?

3. From what you have discovered in this study, how would you explain to a friend why Jesus died?

CONCLUSION

Jesus endured rejection, mockery, false accusations, suffering and death for us. He refused to save himself so that he could save us. How amazing that, like Barabbas, we may live because he died in our place.

How do you respond to such love? Perhaps you can understand the love and gratitude that overflowed from the sinful woman in Simon's house. You may want to ask Jesus for courage to wisely and lovingly answer the questions or accusations of men and women who don't recognize who Jesus is. You may need to ask him to teach you to forgive as he forgives.

DISCUSSION 8

*Distressed Friends and
A Doubter*

JOHN 20:1-31

Remember your deepest loss and the devastating grief that followed. Perhaps it was the loss of a loved one, or a dream, or a hope dashed. Maybe you huddled with others who shared your pain, or maybe you grieved alone. Either way, your world was wrapped in darkness, inside and out.

1. Think about a time of grief in your life. What was helpful to you during your grief, and what was not helpful?

When Jesus was arrested, some of his friends fled for their lives. Others watched him die along with their hope that he was God's promised Messiah. Joseph of Arimathea gained Pilate's permission to remove Jesus' body for burial before the Sabbath. According to Jewish custom, he wrapped the body with spices in strips of linen. In a nearby garden, Joseph placed the body in a new tomb, closed with a large stone over the entrance. Some of the women at the cross followed Joseph and saw the tomb (Luke 23:55-56).

Because the law prohibited traveling on the Sabbath, the women could not go to the tomb until Sunday morning. Imagine their grief as they waited to return to mourn at the tomb.

DISTRESSED FRIENDS
READ JOHN 20:1-18
SCENE 1, SUNDAY MORNING

2. What do you imagine Mary of Magdala is thinking and feeling as she walks to the tomb before dawn?

As she runs to find the disciples?

3. How do the disciples respond to Mary's news (verses 3-8)?

Note: The other disciple is probably John the author of the book.

4. What do Peter or the other disciple see and not see in the tomb?

5. When the other disciple went in he saw and believed. What does he believe?

6. What clearly indicates that the disciples and Mary did not expect Jesus to rise from the dead (verses 9-15)?

7. What do you learn about Jesus from the way he reveals himself to Mary and from his instructions to her in verses 15-17?

8. How do you picture Mary delivering her news and Jesus' message to the disciples (verses 17, 18)?

Note: In Judaism, a woman was not considered a reliable witness, but Jesus sends Mary as the first eyewitness to his resurrection.

READ JOHN 20:19-23
SCENE 2, SUNDAY EVENING

9. Peter and John must have told the other disciples what they saw at the tomb. Later, Mary arrives to announce, "I have seen the Lord!" and tells them Jesus' message. How do you picture the mood and conversations in the room?

10. What do you learn about Jesus' resurrected body from the way he comes to the disciples?

How does Jesus' resurrection change his distressed friends?

How does it change our lives now?

A DOUBTER
READ JOHN 20:24-31
SCENE 3

11. We aren't told why Thomas is not with the other disciples when Jesus appears the first time. Thomas may need to grieve alone. When he does join them, how does Thomas respond to their news (verses 24, 25)?

12. What impresses you about how Jesus confronts Thomas' doubts?

13. What moves Thomas from honest doubt to worshipping Jesus as God?

14. What encouragement do you find here in facing your doubts?

REFLECTION

1. Thomas' choice to believe the evidence about Jesus illustrates the purpose of John's Gospel. What do we need to choose to believe and why (verses 30, 31)?

2. What difference does it make now and eternally if we choose to believe or choose not to believe?

3. Reflect on what you discovered about Jesus in these eight studies. He may have surprised you, confused you, made you uncomfortable, attracted you to him, met your needs. Do you need more of Jesus' grace or more of his truth in your life right now? Explain.

CONCLUSION

The risen Lord Jesus endured the cross and the grave to bring us forgiveness and eternal life. He came to Mary, to the disciples, and to Thomas transforming their grief and doubt to joy. As Jesus did for Thomas he takes our doubts seriously, graciously confronting us with evidence. He gives us the freedom and opportunity to choose to believe.

How do you respond to Jesus? Do you have doubts you want to offer honestly to him? Do you want to thank him for what you have learned in these studies? Do you want to ask him to keep working in your heart to help you make the right choices day by day? Are you willing to declare in words and actions that Jesus is the risen Christ, the Son of God?

If you have appreciated these studies, you can discover more about Jesus from one of his biographies in the New Testament, the gospel of Mark.
You may order from Neighborhood Bible Studies, 1-800-369-0307 or www.neighborhoodbiblestudy.org.

WHAT SHOULD OUR GROUP STUDY NEXT?

We recommend the Gospel of Mark, the fast paced narrative of Jesus' life, as the first book for people new to Bible study. Follow this with the Book of Acts to see what happens to the people introduced in Mark. Then in Genesis discover the beginnings of the world and find the answers to the big questions of where we came from and why we are here.

Our repertoire of guides allows great flexibility. For groups starting with *Lenten Studies, They Met Jesus* is a good sequel.

LEVEL 101: little or no previous Bible study experience
Mark (recommended first unit of study) or The Book of Mark
  (Simplified English)
Acts, Books 1 and 2
Genesis, Books 1 and 2
Psalms/Proverbs
Topical Studies
Conversations with Jesus
Lenten Studies
Foundations for Faith
Character Studies
They Met Jesus

> **Sequence for groups reaching people from non-Christian cultures**
> Foundations for Faith
> Genesis, Books 1 and 2
> Mark, Discovering Jesus *or* The Book of Mark
> *(Simplified English)*

LEVEL 201: some experience in Bible study (after 3-4 Level 101 books)

John, Books 1 and 2	Treasures
Romans	Relationships
I John/James	Servants of the Lord
1 Corinthians	Coping with Stress
2 Corinthians	Work – God's Gift
Philippians	Celebrate
Colossians	*Character Studies*
Topical Studies	Four Men of God
Prayer	Lifestyles of Faith, Books 1 and 2

LEVEL 301: More experienced in Bible study

Matthew, Books 1 and 2	*Topical Studies*
Galatians & Philemon	Set Free
1 and 2 Peter	
Hebrews	***Biweekly or Monthly Groups*
1 and 2 Thessalonians, 2 & 3	*may use topical studies or*
John	*character studies.*
Isaiah	
Ephesians	

ABOUT NEIGHBORHOOD BIBLE STUDIES

Neighborhood Bible Studies, Inc. is a leader in the field of small group Bible studies. Since 1960, NBS has pioneered the development of Bible study groups that encourage each member to participate in the leadership of the discussion.

The mission of Neighborhood Bible Studies is to:
>Enable people to investigate the Scriptures
>Encounter God in Jesus Christ
>Mature in their faith

The vision of Neighborhood Bible Studies is to:
>Change the World
>One neighborhood at a time
>Through the study of the Bible

Publication in more than 20 languages indicates the versatility of NBS cross culturally. NBS methods and materials are used around the world to:
>Equip individuals for facilitating discovery Bible studies
>Serve as a resource to the church

Skilled NBS personnel provide consultation by telephone or e-mail. In some areas, they conduct workshops and seminars to train individuals, clergy, and laity in how to establish small group Bible studies in neighborhoods, churches, workplaces and specialized facilities. Call 1-800-369-0307 to inquire about consultation or training.

ABOUT THE FOUNDERS

Marilyn Kunz and Catherine Schell, authors of many of the NBS guides, founded Neighborhood Bible Studies and directed its work for thirty-one years. Currently other authors contribute to the series.

The cost of your study guide has been subsidized by faithful people who give generously to NBS. For more information, visit our web site: www.neighbohoodbiblestudy.org 1-800-369-0307

COMPLETE LISTING OF NBS STUDY GUIDES

Getting Started
How to Start a Neighborhood Bible Study *(handbook & video/audio cassette)*

Bible Book Studies
Genesis, Book 1 *Begin with God*
Genesis, Book 2 *Discover Your Roots*
Psalms & Proverbs *Journals of Wisdom*
Isaiah *God's Help Is on the Way*
Matthew, Book 1 *God's Promise Kept*
Matthew, Book 2 *God's Purpose Fulfilled*
Mark *Discover Jesus*
Luke *Good News and Great Joy*
John, Book 1 *Believe and See*
John, Book 2 *Believe and Live*
Acts, Book 1 *The Holy Spirit Transforms Lives*
Acts, Book 2 *Amazing Journeys with God*
Romans *A Reasoned Faith*
1 Corinthians *Finding Answers to Life's Questions*
2 Corinthians *The Power in Weakness*
Galatians & Philemon *Fully Accepted by God*
Ephesians *God's Design for Relationships*
Philippians *A Message of Encouragement*
Colossians *Staying Focused on Truth*
1 & 2 Thessalonians, 2 & 3 John, Jude *The Coming of the Lord*
Hebrews *Access to God*
1 & 2 Peter *Strength Amidst Stress*
1 John & James *Faith that Lives*

Topical Studies
Celebrate *Reasons for Hurrahs*
Conversations with Jesus *Intimate Snapshots*
Change *Facing the Unexpected*
Foundations for Faith *The Basics for Knowing God*
Lenten Studies *Life Defeats Death*
Prayer *Communicating with God*
Relationships *Connect to Others: God's Plan*
Servants of the Lord *Embrace God's Agenda*
Set Free *Leaving Negative Emotions Behind*
Treasures *Discover God's Riches*
Work - God's Gift *Life-Changing Choices*

Character Studies
Four Men of God *Lessons in Obedience*
Moses *Learning to Lead*
Lifestyles of Faith, Book One *Choosing to Trust God*
Lifestyles of Faith, Book Two *Choosing to Obey God*
They Met Jesus *Life-Changing Encounters*

Simplified English
The Book of Mark *The Story of Jesus*

55 / CONVERSATIONS WITH JESUS